AS EASY AS BUSINESS

SHAZ JONES

ISBN:
978-1-6959-0125-4

DEDICATION

To all my amazing clients who've invited me

to create profits with them.

CONTENTS

1 INTRODUCTION

Every week my work is to work with the best and brightest business owners to create the fastest path to profit. Sometimes this is so fast it makes their head spin. Then they get cranky! Not at me – at themselves, for wasting years, sometimes decades, doing things on their own, the hard way, and not asking for help.

I've had my own business (Onliners.com.au) for more than 25 years. And over that time I've served clients who are owners of just about every business possible – from gold mines to Antarctica travel to cleaners to television shopping networks.

Nearly all of them thought their business was complicated when I met them. They thought it was difficult. And their business was different from every other business in history.

When you think business is hard it will be hard. If you

think its complex, it will be. You'll struggle, you'll work harder and longer than you need to, and you'll expect the same of your staff, suppliers and you may even make things hard for you customers.

You'll be drawn to courses, consultants and gurus who can analyse all the diversity for you and help you battle through the minefield of disaster awaiting you. You'll be a sucker for stress-relieving products and services... and it may even start to take its toll on you physically and emotionally.

I thought business was hard, too, when I first started my own business.

But the way I see it now, nothing could be easier!

I've learnt to see business differently. Whilst some can't see the wood for the detailed trees, and others never plant enough trees because they're too busy dreaming about the vast woods, I've learnt to look away from the woods and the trees.

Just the same as some can't see the purpose for all the pain, and others can disregard the pain in pursuit of a higher purpose, I've learnt to look past the pain and the purpose and find the profit beyond both.

My purpose for going through the pain of writing another book is that you'll discover how easy business can be when you can see the fastest path to profit.

2 SEVERAL STEPS TO SEVERAL HUNDRED MILLION DOLLARS

At first glance, it's not an easy business.

In early 2019, I started working with a television shopping network that broadcasts 24 hours a day, every day of the year across international borders and on both free to air and subscription TV services. Many of the over 100,000 products are sourced from around the world and must undergo a rigorous quality assurance process to ever be shown on television. Some products are ingested (like protein powders) and some are put on skin (like makeup) and can have horrible physical consequences if they are not of the highest standards. Even if they are passed by the quality assurance process and meet all of the government requirements for sales in public, the sales scripts may fail the hurdles that the lawyers create for making "defensible" claims in the public marketplace. Then there are all the ordinary problems of a thriving 9 figure business; human resources, stock control, distribution, finance, marketing and so on.

The most pressing problem of the business though was that the customers that had been their loyal buyers for almost twenty years, were now aging and spending less and they weren't attracting new, younger customers.

A smart lady with boundless energy, Judy had just reached the pinnacle of her career so far and been made General Manager after more than 20 years in the industry. She loves her job and has a great relationship with many of her suppliers (who she helps to make millions of dollars a year). And she especially enjoys social media. You'll find her on Instagram and Facebook at all hours of the day and night.

Judy was used to working long hours, managing complexity and responding quickly to rapid change. But Judy had no idea how to turn over 100,000 products and a television business model generating hundreds of millions of dollars every year into social media sales before she met me. In fact, when we first started working together, she assumed if she didn't know then I certainly wouldn't know either!

Judy assumed the solution would be complex. And to tell you the truth, I hadn't solved that particular problem before, and at first it looked like she might just be right.

But using the simple 7 step method that I unfold in this book, I discovered an easy path to social media sales that generated hundreds of thousands of dollars in just a few hours. The ongoing cost is zero, zip, zilch, nada, nothing (unlike the broadcast television model which can easily cost a six figure sum every hour), and the revenue and profits are unlimited and timeless.

The solution was so elegant it only required one line of code to create an automated social sales cash machine that will constantly refresh itself each hour with the products that are most attractive to brand new customers right now.

As those meerkats in the ad say, "Simples".

Every business I've ever encountered, whether a brand new one-person startup, or an aging multi-million dollar international corporation, is easy when you know how to find the fastest path to profit.

So let's get started!

SHAZ JONES

3 STEP 1 - F

When you woke up today you had the same opportunity as everyone else on the planet to manage your own time and energy.

You also had similar constraints that limited you. We can't (yet) physically clone ourselves to be in multiple places doing multiple things at one time. So we have to choose how we spend our one allocation of time.

Warren Buffett, the richest investor in the history of the planet, tells a story of when he met the father of Bill Gates. At the time Bill Gates was the richest person on the planet, and Warren Buffett as the richest investor wasn't far behind him – just a billion or so short.

Mr Gates Senior asked both Bill and Warren to separately write down on a piece of paper what one factor had helped them the most to be so successful in life.

They both write the same thing. Just one word.

FOCUS

Focus is the one skill that allows your success at every other thing to accumulate and grow. And it's this compound progress that the world's richest people invest in every day that most others never do.

I like to think of focus as the opposite of the hokey-pokey. In the game of hokey pokey children follow along to the song.

You put your right foot in

You put your right foot out

You put your right foot in

And you shake it all about

You do the hokey pokey

And you turn around

That's what its all about.

This seven step process is then repeated over and over again (with the left foot, the right arm, the left arm and so on).

When the hokey pokey ends, the children have completed the seven step process multiple times.

And they are still in the same spot.

Whilst this is a great game for entertaining children when you need to keep them in the one spot, sadly many adults play a similar game when it comes to their business. They are continually busy. And make no progress at all.

Imagine if one woman does several rounds of the hokey pokey each day, while another woman instead takes 7 steps in the one direction, several times a day.

Whilst they will both invest the same amount of time and energy, the first woman will make no progress at all, whilst the second woman will be getting closer to her goal every day.

But even if you've decided to focus, what do you focus on?

This is what I call a "Leverage Point".

Now imagine a third woman who takes those steps not just in the same horizontal direction, but she also adds another dimension and climbs a staircase. Now she is taking the same amount of steps but making compound progress in two dimensions with every step she takes. She'll not only arrive at her (horizontal) goal faster, but she'll be at a completely different level when she gets there.

Leverage is why some focused people get far better results than others.

Did you know that the amount of revenue from all of the e-commerce websites in Australia for a whole year, are less than the amount of revenue from just one of the e-commerce websites in China on just one day of the year?

Differences in results like these happen all the time. So you have to become good at spotting them.

Here's the basic skill (yes, it can easily be learned). You analyse the inputs versus the outputs.

You're looking for the least amount of inputs versus the maximum outputs.

In business, we would normally measure both the inputs and outputs in dollar terms. So if you are selling soap and it costs you $1 to buy it from your supplier and deliver it to your client, how much can you charge your client for that? If they are only prepared to pay $1 for it, this is not a good use of your time, energy or dollars. This is called a "proportionate" result. For every unit of input, you receive back a return of the same amount. This zero profit break-even mentality is how many people run their business. They stay in "survival mode" barely eking out a living their whole life. They get cash in from their client, and pay it straight back out to their suppliers. They are doing the cash hokey pokey and they end up getting nowhere in life.

But if clients are willing to pay you $4 for it, multiplying your dollars four times every "step" might be a very good business decision. This is called a "disproportionate" result – the portion of inputs don't equal the same portion of outputs. Now with every transaction you make, you are heading faster and faster into profit mode.

If you can find a client who is willing to pay you $4 and wants to buy a lot, the high profit and high volume will accelerate your business profits faster and higher.

Look for minimum input and maximum output; small actions, big reactions.

Begin practicing just in daily conversations. Often the

less you say (minimum input) turns out to give the best reaction (maximum output). Simply saying "I love you" might mean more than a whole hour spent lecturing the person... weird thing to say to your client, though 😉

When you learn to focus your time and energy on leverage points, you'll get much better results than even highly focused people. And you'll achieve your goals a lot faster and easier, like a snowball growing naturally as it hurtles downhill.

Once I start working with people they find that they are growing too quick, and harnessing that momentum becomes their only "problem".

When I first met Cassie she had an idea. And nothing else. She'd never started a business before. She didn't have a business name, business model, business plan or even a bank account. Nothing. Within three months her idea had turned into a business snowball growing so quickly she emailed me saying "I think I'm making too much money".

Now that's a problem I can definitely help with!

Almost a decade later, she's since married and had her first child and is still crushing it in her business by the way.

So what goal do you want to focus on?

For many people this is a set amount of money, or

maybe something money can do for you, like a new car or an overseas holiday or creating the dream lifestyle. But trust me those goals can be achieved really quickly. And in the end they don't really motivate you.

You want your goal to be long-term... so long-term you might even think it's unachievable right now.

But before you get into what your future long-term goal is, one of the best exercises to do is to look back the other way.

Who do you think you are?

Who did you want to be when you were younger? What things came easier to you or meant more to you than others your age? Especially look at the time before you started school – because gifts are things you are born with, you can't learn them at school, you can only learn to refine them.

Whilst my two brothers loved running around outside and playing active and interactive games like "cops and robbers" or "cowboys and Indians", I preferred to sit in the once spot on my own and read and think for hours on end. Long before I'd even been inside a classroom, I would daydream about being a teacher and having others listen to me.

I was born with an unlearned gift to learn. I used to like learning. I'm still insatiably curious about almost everything. I was always asking adults "why?". Whilst nearly every child goes through this phase, mine was much more intense and prolonged than other children. Nearly every adult would comment on it when they met me. What they didn't see is whenever I felt I understood a subject, I would hold a class with all my dolls as students. And I still love learning and sharing knowledge now (which is part of the reason why I write books).

Sometimes, especially when things come really easy to us, we assume it must be as natural for everyone. But that's rarely the case. So a useful question to ponder is what were the things that stood out about you to others? I was chatting with one of my artist clients recently and her parents noticed her gifting in this area when she was just four years old.

Another story my parents and siblings used to tell everyone about happened before I started school. I couldn't add up or multiply or divide, I could barely count. But I worked out a way to buy lollies cheap and sell them to my brother at twice the price. I had managed to identify a commercial opportunity with 100% markup margin before I could literally add two and two together. Business has always come easy to me!

For some, it might only find expression when you are with other people – this is particularly true of the social and caring gifts. Who do you like to help? Choosing your target field can be very powerful. The market will always be bigger than your target. You might aim at helping female solo entrepreneurs and end up also helping male executives at large corporates, and that's fine. But knowing who your target is makes business a lot easier.

I somehow knew that my target field should be business people, not lovers of lollies. I don't think even opening up a global chain of candy stores would have satisfied my intellectual curiosity like working with hundreds of clients on the cutting edge of technology has (but it sure has funded my enduring love of lollies).

Some of the most inspirational business owners I know started their business by solving a problem they had personally experienced. It might be trivial or tragic but "scratching your own itch" is another path that people hone their focus. One man I know had a dust allergy and now has a successful cleaning business. Another young lady I know could never find swimwear she liked and now has a global fashion label.

One woman might really enjoy numbers and make a great accountant mixing with celebrities during long breaks on film sets, while another woman might have the same gift but find Hollywood superficial and the long breaks unproductive and boring. Instead she may love helping the elderly manage their finances to set them up for success in retirement. Whilst both women have the same gift for numbers, the field they choose to use their gift in will have a profound effect on their job satisfaction.

For others your genius might only function when you are in the right environment. Birds look so majestic when they are gliding in the sky. And whales are magnificent when they are in the ocean. Where do you shine? What environments make you look good?

Note, this might not always be an obvious place that you enjoy being. For example, I love technology and feel really at home in front of a computer. But I actually shine when I'm with a group of people who know nothing about computers. When my technology skills are soaring high above theirs, they think I'm a genius! And whilst I wouldn't hang out with all of my technology clients if they weren't paying me, I do enjoy the feeling of being valued and having my gifts recognised and appreciated.

Remember, if you start a business, you're going to be helping these people for years, probably decades and possibly your entire life. If you hate your field, you won't be motivated and probably won't end up very good at your job. But if you can find a way to like your field, or choose a different field that you do like, work won't feel like work it will feel like a privilege. So don't start a business to help people lose weight – no matter how good your idea is - if you don't know anyone struggling with their weight and don't like spending time with them.

Pay attention to where you shine and are valued and feel motivated to share your gifts with others. Make your goal about helping those people, and you'll find the long-term payoff will be far better than a new car or a great holiday.

Once you know your goal, you'll know what feedback to pay attention to. Remain focused on taking steps in that one direction and assess whether you are getting closer to that goal or not.

How many likes you get on Instagram is most likely completely unrelated to your goal. Watching the news every night or the latest season of The Bachelor is probably going to be a giant waste of time that doesn't provide value to anyone else or get you any closer to your goal.

Make it a habit to eliminate wasted time and energy, and focus on your goal of creating value for others.

Remember, when you wake up tomorrow you'll have the same opportunity to manage your time and energy as everyone else. And there'll be all sorts of hokey pokey distractions and temptations along the way. But if you want to take the fastest path to profit, you'll do more of what works and less of what doesn't. Ironically, the better you get at focusing, the more you'll feel like you're doing less. Because you will be doing less hokey pokey going nowhere, but getting more compound progress towards your goal. More, with less. That's the power of focus.

4 STEP 2 – A

Now that you know what your gift is, what field you are going to pursue to meet your goal, it's time to get the attention of your target market.

To do that you need to service them in a way that creates real value for them. And the way to do that is to look at what they're not getting right now. What is their biggest pain point or their most regular problem? Where are the gaps in the current services or products they're purchasing?

The more agonising that problem is, the easier it will be to get their attention when you provide a solution. Look for the agony.

One error that business owners make in this area is thinking they have to solve every problem for their target market. You don't. You don't even have to solve a whole problem. You can solve a tiny slice of a problem, especially when you are first starting out.

Being hungry, especially for a long time can be physically agonising. At first it might just be the mental distraction that you need to eat, or a gurgle in your tummy or a mild cramp. But the longer it goes on the more emotional and all-consuming it can be. Obviously, left long enough, starvation can be deadly.

McDonalds solves the problem of hunger. But it doesn't solve every problem for everyone who is hungry, every time they're hungry. In fact, each day McDonald's only serves meals to about one percent of the world's population (about 70 million people). But if you live close to a McDonald's restaurant, and you feel like a Big Mac, fries and Coke, their whole business is set up to solve that slice of the hunger problem for you.

What slice of what problem can you solve for your target market? Even if you only solve it for your customers 1 in every 100 times they have the problem, like McDonalds, you'll probably still have a really good business.

Some business owners try to be all things to all people and end up satisfying no-one. This is especially true for businesses that have been around for a while. They may start out with just one service, but a favourite client asks them to do something else, so they add that service. Then another, and another. They end up with too many moving parts. Over the years their business gets very complex and they end up like a juggler with six balls in the air and they can't see anyway to stop without the whole thing coming crashing down. But how do you streamline processes and simplify the overall business throughput if your business is already established?

I prefer the Goldilocks approach. When she was hungry, Goldilocks tasted all three bowls of porridge before deciding on which one to eat. The first was too hot, the second was too cold, but the third bowl was "just right" and she ate it all up.

If you hate selling, don't focus on the sales-related problems of your target market, or find an automated way to do sales. Or if you hate paper-work, don't focus on the administration problems of your target market. Try out a few different solutions that work well for both you and your target market. Your business will always feel uncomfortable for you until you find the slice of the problem that is "just right".

It's no secret that the bigger the problem you solve, the more money you can make. If you take someone's rubbish away for them they may pay you a small amount. But if you take a brain tumour away for them, they will value that a lot more highly. And you'll have to be a lot more skilled. Personal, permanent, complex health problems are far more agonising than a bag of rubbish every Tuesday.

Of course, other things being equal, you'll make more money if you can solve their problem regularly. Obviously, you can't do that with brain tumours. But if the product or service you are providing is of low value, like rubbish removal or cleaning services, you can make it of higher value by providing it more frequently.

You can also make your product or service of higher value by thinking a bit laterally. Turn your competitors into your customers.

In just about every industry, training others to earn a living is more highly valued than actually providing that service. So look for opportunities to show others in the industry what you are already doing to relive the agony of your customers. Rubbish removal and cleaning aren't that complex but there are always new techniques (e.g. for recycling), new equipment, machinery, technology, products or even tax laws, business finance and insurances that you can educate others about and generate a new stream of income whilst establishing yourself as the expert in your industry.

Another way to attract attention of customers is simply to get more customers. All of your customers can become referrers for you, especially if you explicitly ask them to. Some business owners I talk to get worried that serving more customers will "dilute" their value. But the opposite is true. Serving more customers strengthens your value. Don't see adding customers as adding water which will weaken your secret sauce, but rather see each new customer as another drop of concentrate that will replenish your secret sauce.

Marketing, and in particular advertising, is the best way to capture attention of new customers. There are many studies that show advertised products are seen as better than their equal unadvertised products. Indeed, for many products they are made in the same factory with the same ingredients using the same process, but the advertised brand can command much higher prices.

Why? Because they have captured the attention of their customers. If I ask 100 people what they think of when I say "hamburger" more than 90 of them will say McDonalds. It's not because they make the best hamburgers in the world, its because they make the most hamburgers in the world. And they do that, by consistently advertising to attract the attention of customers.

This is also the reason why the winner of a talent show will earn many times the amount of income after winning the talent show as they did before. Their talent is the same, but they have captured the attention of more people, so their value is higher.

Love him or hate him Donald Trump is very skilful at attracting attention. In fields as diverse as residential real estate, golf course design, casinos, beauty pageants, reality tv show, and even as a Presidential candidate, it could be argued that the only real value he provided was attracting attention. So valuable is that skill that it took him all the way to becoming the most powerful man in the world.

If you look at your business like a garden hose where you turn on a tap of $1 water drops in at one end and out the other end you produce $4 drops, you're going to need to find a steady flow of customers who are willing to pay you $4.

One of the simplest definitions I ever heard of business is "Businesses is finding someone to pay you enough for something so that you can do it again". It doesn't necessarily mean you do it again for them, but you can afford to do it again for someone. It's a simple profit formula: revenue-expenses=profits. As long as you can find someone to pay you more revenue than it cost you in expenses, you can make profits.

A lot of people can do that once, but they struggle to find a predictable, reliable, sustainable way to produce profits. And the first major problem they encounter is like a blockage in their garden hose. I hate it when you're trying to water the garden and suddenly the hose gets a kink in it that stops the flow of water entirely, or at least retards it down to a trickle. The first kink in business is usually the inability to predictably attract attention from potential customers.

When your business is running well, advertising is one of the best returns on investment you will ever get. And it's the fastest way I know to deliver you a steady stream of customers.

If you put your money in the bank you might only get 1 or 2% return if you leave it there for an entire year. If you take on a bit more risk and put it in the stock market your returns will be less predictable but might be a bit higher, even up to double figures like 10-12% in a good year. But the potential returns from advertising can easily be 100-200% and more. Advertising is one of those leverage points that starts your business taking forward steps up, getting your business to a much higher level as you get closer to your goal.

And yet I find a lot of business owners are scared to invest in advertising.

Usually this is because they've tried advertising before and "it didn't work". In almost every case I've seen this is because the business owner has advertised too early. When you don't know yet what the agony point for your customer is, you will waste all of your advertising budget producing ads that don't resonate with your target market.

When I was younger I went travelling around Scotland with a few friends. One of the guys had bought a cheap car that we all piled into every day to do our sight seeing. It wasn't a luxurious ride, but it always got us from point A to point B. The only problem was you couldn't start it with the key. We'd have to park it on a downward slope with a clear run in front of us, so we could get behind it and push start it each time. Once we heard the engine kick in, the driver would brake and let us all jump in before we drove off.

I liken advertising to that push-start. You've got to know that the car will work fine after you give it that initial push. Don't ever ask advertising to do the whole journey. Some business owners even expect it to create the car!

You have to setup your business for success first by making sure you've got a good car, with a clear run and a downward slope before you give it a push with advertising, otherwise you are just wasting your money.

When you know what the agony point is for your customers, they will already be searching for a solution. So they will self-qualify as soon as you capture their attention.

If you haven't yet figured out what the biggest pain point is for your target market, ask them. I like to keep asking why – sometimes five or more times. For example, if I'm talking to a business owner and they identify their biggest problem is having no new customers I ask why that's a problem. They may say because they can't afford to invest in new technology unless they get new customers. So again I ask why. They may say because they tried to get a loan for new technology but the bank refused them. Again, I ask why.

They may say that they refused to pay a supplier once who sent them bad products and got a black mark on their credit report.

Getting a deeper understanding of your customer's pain points it's one of the best investments any business owner can make. It's amazing how when you ask why a few times, your investigation uncovers entirely new and otherwise unrelated problems. Now I know that the root cause of this customer's problem has nothing to do with advertising or customers or technology or finance. They just need to learn how to better resolve issues with their suppliers so it never happens again, and then clean up their credit report.

If I hadn't asked why, I might have spent months of time and millions of dollars creating ads, and yet never really solving their agony. I would've wasted my time, energy, money – and theirs too. I would probably come to the false conclusion that advertising doesn't work.

Now that I know the real problem, I can eliminate all that waste, and just focus on providing real value.

It can feel uncomfortable at first to keep asking why – both for you and your potential customer. But please persist. It's the easiest way I know to uncover the real agony point so I can't start doing more of what works and less of what doesn't, to provide real value to my customers.

Taking this second step into a deeper understanding of

the agony of your customer, might just help you capture the attention of the world one day, and you won't need orange hair and millions of followers on Twitter to do it.

5 STEP 3 - S

Step three is all about solutions. How can you solve the slice of the problem you've decided to solve? Often this will involve something that you are uniquely qualified to see or source. Bill Gates saw the coming personal computer revolution long before others did. Steve Jobs saw the same thing that others were missing. But Bill Gates could see the "invisible" part software would play, whereas Steve Jobs initially focused more on the look and feel of the hardware.

What things are you aware of that no-one else seems to be paying attention to? Do you have a passion or a skill that you can bring to bear on a problem that hasn't been solved yet or that you would solve differently?

For business to be easy, it has to suit YOU – your personality, your giftings, your lifestyle. And that will be different for everyone.

I'm not the first one to see that writing books is a way to help business owners manage their businesses differently. Literally millions of others have written business books before me. But I have a unique way of seeing business that makes it easy for even first-time entrepreneurs to get started in business.

Often the most successful businesses are those that combine an old problem with a new solution Some problems we humans seem to always develop (e.g. back pain, weight gain) and because different people respond differently we also develop new ways of dealing with the problem. If the one diet worked for everyone, we wouldn't need another diet book. There's no perfect solution yet, so if you can see a new way of structuring our eating patterns, why not share it with the world?

Later on I'll walk you through how to iiterate and experiment with your solution, so it doesn't have to be perfect at this stage (if every). But getting something that a group of customers respond positively too is the goal here. If they respond so positively they spontaneously share it with others who have the same problem, or would like to use it in the same way, you know you're probably on a winner.

One of my previous employees has moved to Vietnam and started a business. She's a very talented designer and has travelled the world researching textiles and design across multiple cultures. But when I saw her social media launch my heart sank. It looked beautiful…. But there was no offer. There was a lot of information about Saigon and her suppliers and fabrics and the new business and ideas and supporters and … no offer.

If you don't take anything else from this book, remember this:
No Offer = No Customers = No Profits!

Unfortunately, they're still just sharing good news about the people they were collaborating with and the new fabrics they had available. But there's been no news of customers yet, and sadly, I'm not surprised.

Can you imagine if real estate agents never showed you a house or told you the price, but just kept showing you a brick here, and a piece of carpet there ... and a new window frame type ... sure that might be interesting to some people – but its not the same as selling a house.

Craft an offer that people can say "yes" too ...

People say no to what confuses them ... what are they actually selling? How much will it cost? How do they even price? What will I have to pay extra for? Will I have to buy a minimum order?

Don't try and answer all of the questions (but at least be aware that people may ask those questions. Put them all in an FAQ doc).

Use this simple format:

X for $y

Look at a k-mart catalogue ... this top for this amount (sizes range from ... comes in these colours, sale ends on this date). Simple.

Just have one solution per offer … don't try and be all things to all people.

Like a maths problem, there are many, many wrong answers, but there's only one right answer. When your offer is clearly about one thing, people have the confidence to say yes or no.

No one likes to feel uncertain or stupid … so if they don't immediately get it, they'll usually say no and move on rather than risk appearing silly by asking questions…

Your job is to remove complexity … some business owners think its their job to give their clients as many options as possible. Nope. In fact, if a client has too many options they tend to say no to all of them. Analysis paralysis. Your job is to help your client make an informed purchasing decision. That doesn't mean they need a hundred different facts. You need to simplify the facts down to just the bare minimum … x for $y is about as simple as it gets.

Imagine if a real estate agent tried to sell a house by telling the client where the sand came from that went into making the window. That's a fact. It's unique to this house. But the buyer doesn't need (or want) to know that when they are deciding if they should invest their life savings to make this their new home. Edit yourself – especially if you're a detail person. Assess every detail. Share only enough details to help them feel confident about making the purchase decision.

Guarantee and refunds policy can help instill trust ... but don't get caught up in all the fine print of terms and conditions before you are clear on a single, simple, solution. This step-by-step guide is about the fastest path to profits, not the most comprehensive legal paperwork. Of course, I want you to comply with all legal requirements. But never ask a lawyer if you need more legal terms. That's like asking a hairdresser if you need a haircut. They'll always say yes.

Keep your solution simple if you want it to be as easy as business.

6 STEP 4 - T

Tests are designed not just to see if you've learned knowledge and skills, but also how well you can assess new situations and apply that knowledge and skills.

On the final test police recruits are asked what they'd do if ordered to arrest their own mother.

One recruit wrote "Call for backup"!

I'm not sure he ever passed the test.

Your business is going to depend on your ability to test the market and assess how your new product fits. Will the market ignore it or lap it up? Will they pay even more than you thought or nothing at all?

The more thoroughly test your product-market fit at this early stage, the more heartache you will save yourself down the track.

You need to be humble enough to lay down your own opinions and gather real evidence of demand, pricing and every other factor that is changeable about your product and market.

This is not the time to go with your gut-feel. This is not the time to only ask friends or family. You want truly independent people. Don't get me wrong, it's okay to start with friends and family, and ask them to introduce you to their friends and family. But ultimately the best type of person is someone who is prepared to be rude to you – and brutally honest about your solution.

You don't want to know if they like the colour, or think it's too expensive at this stage, you just want to know if it solves the problem you are trying to solve.

There are several ways to test your solution. The best way is to go out to meet the public – hang outside a shopping centre or a railway station or a city corner at peak hour, carry a clipboard, and ask people to answer a couple of quick questions. You'll very quickly learn how completely disinterested in you the general public are.

You'll learn how to capture their attention. You'll learn what they will and won't spend time and money on. It will bruise your ego – and that's a good thing, because you can't pay a mortgage with your ego. You'll find something far more useful than ego – profits!

If you can get one or two of them to actually test out

your solution, not just answer questions, even better! If you can devise an online or offline way to get them to choose between two options (never, ever, test more than one thing at a time), you'll rapidly speed up your understanding of your market.

If you can let them take home a sample to try at home, or ask them to download something online in exchange for their honest feedback, you're on your way to getting great test results.

Like a detective building a case against the shrewdest criminal masterminds, you must be prepared to spend the time and energy to find out the truth, not just confirm your own prejudices. Detectives are always on the lookout to identify several factors. For example, in a murder case, you need a means – i.e. a weapon, opportunity, motive, and of course identify a suspect.

But that's only the start, you still need to find witnesses, examine CCTV footage, question the suspect, confirm an alibi, match physical evidence that ties the suspect to the crime scene... in other words you need to test your theories. People's lives may depend on your testing.

In your business, your financial future at the very least, will depend on your testing. So do not skip this step!

7 STEP 5 - E

Evolving your product is essential. Your first attempt is not going to be perfect. In fact, you may *never* get to perfect. But you can start heading in that direction.

And that's the key – start heading in that direction.

Don't sit here and wait until you have something perfect, or you will never get anywhere.

You need to keep iterating; improving on just one thing at a time.

Why? Because you can't do valid testing unless you are only testing one thing at a time. If you change several things and it starts selling more, or worse, starts selling less, how do you know which change is causing the difference?

Your aim should be to create something that "sells

itself". The nirvana is for people to see it once and say "where do I get one?"

Just yesterday I was looking for something to buy my mum for her next birthday. She's turning 80 in a few weeks. I was looking at all kinds of things from iPads to fancy walking sticks. Then I saw a phone (she still has a landline) that had large buttons (she's had a stroke and her right hand isn't as agile as it used to be) where you could slide in photos. So she would be able to ring up each of her kids, and grandkids (her great grandkids are too young to talk on the phone yet) by just pressing two buttons.

I never knew I wanted it, because I didn't even know it existed, until I saw it. But as soon as I saw it, I wanted to click through from this website and buy a photo phone on Amazon.

Forget about whether people need your product, or even if they want your product. There's a big difference between what people need, want, and are prepared to buy.

I haven't ever needed a BMW. But for decades I wanted a BMW but wasn't prepared to buy one. As the value of my home started increasing, I'd start reminding myself, I could sell this home today and buy myself my dream BMW. The day came when I could buy two BMWs if I sold my home. Then the day came when I could pay my mortgage and pay off a BMW. Yet every month I would

keep paying more on my mortgage instead of buying a
BMW.

But at a certain point I was finally prepared to buy a
BMW.

A lot of that is simply about timing. That's why you need
to be prepared to let your relationships evolve, not just
your products. Not every potential customer is an actual
customer on day one. It might take decades before they
are prepared to buy from you. But if you keep
improving both your product and relationship with
them (i.e. sending emails that add value to their life),
you'll be increasing the chances of a sale on both fronts.

8 STEP 6 – S

Now it's time to Scale.

This step is step six for a reason. I meet some entrepreneurs and they want to take this step from day one. And it's not wrong to be thinking about it from day one. But you shouldn't be doing it, until you have nailed the other five steps. Your testing should be showing that your product has evolved to a point where it "sells itself" with your target market.

Scale is about moving beyond your target market into ever-increasing markets. It may be the same demographic (i.e. 80 year old mums having a birthday), but in different geographic markets (i.e. in America as well as Australia). Or it might be to different people in the same country.

It was 50 years ago that man landed on the moon and Neil Armstrong said those immortal words "one small step for man, one giant leap for mankind".

I encourage you to think about small steps first instead of giant leaps. For example, if you are using geography to expand, have a strategy to add one state or one country at a time, instead of a giant "go global" aim. Start with the geography that is closest to what is already working, and then test your approach again. You'll quickly learn that every market is different in some way, so you want to focus on the things that are the same.

I have clients that worry about scale. Artists, in particular, seem to be worried about "diluting" their value. This raises an important distinction. You don't have to saturate a market before you scale. Scaling means adding another market. That market might have 5,000,000 potential customers. But that doesn't mean you need to supply 5,000,000 products. You might decide to supply only 5.

Street artist Banksy, has sold art on a global scale, but it is far from mass-market.

Although he has commercial success in some countries, in other countries, his art is more like social work – one graffiti on a wall protesting a political point, that makes no money for him at all directly, yet it serves as a powerful promotion for his other works.

He has an agency which authenticates and sells his commercial works. He has directed a film and written a book (published by Random House in 2005). A year ago he sold a work for one million British pounds (about 1.8 million Aussie dollars). The art work instantly shredded itself. Just a year before that he sold a work for 200,000 Bristish pounds ($365,000), and donated the money to charity.

Most struggling artists see adding a new market like adding water to their coffee – a dilution that weakens the effectiveness. But Banksy and other successful artists see adding a new market like adding an extra shot to their coffee – a concentration that strengthens their effectiveness.

Each new shot, all around the world, is brewing up more power for you. You don't have to keep all those profits for yourself if you don't want to – you can donate them to charity, or even work free of charge. But you will strengthen your brand each time you add a new market.

Value comes from adding more people who come into contact with your work, whether that's through a news headline, or getting their hands on your actual product. Restricting the number of people who even know about your work is the real dilution you should fear.

9 STEP 7 - T

Taking profits is ironically the fastest path to profit only if you wait till the end. If you try and extract profits too soon, you'll end up starving your business of the iron lung it needs to stay alive and grow. You have to be patient until it can breathe on its own. That may be the time when you have hired other people to run the business for you, and are able to extract profits week to week on every product sold, or an annual dividend after you've been to visit your accountant and lodged your tax return for the year. Or it may be when you have your biggest pay day of all, one fat cheque when you sell the business.

Again, the sequence is important. Step seven must be the final, and usually the easiest, of the steps. This is especially true if you have designed what people call a "lifestyle" business for themselves. This intentional strategy not to scale too much, and to keep the business at a size where it only needs one or possibly two (often a husband and wife) to run the business, should still have a profit-taking step.

As I'm writing today is the 21st birthday of Google. In the beginning they weren't making any profit. They didn't even have a plan to make any revenue. It was just two college buddies in a garage with a new idea. But they focused on the first steps, and today, they make about $30,000,000 in profits every day.

Not every business will make that much in profits. In fact, some businesses which end up being the most profitable, may not look like they are successful at all.

The father of one of my friends had a shoe repair shop for decades. It hardly ever made a decent profit, barely enough to pay the mortgages on his home and his shop. He would only work 10-4 each weekday, "repairing soles", which allowed him to eat breakfast and dinner with the family, and drop his kids off at school when they were younger, and spend as much time on the weekends with them as they wanted. As they got older and started getting higher-paying jobs themselves, they would tease him and suggest he sell his little shop, and "get a real job". When he turned 60, and all of his children had left home and got good jobs, he sold his business – it had done it's job.

The business still wasn't worth much in its own right. But the retail premises had more than doubled in value many times over the decades and pushed the price of the business well over the million dollar mark. He and his wife have kept the home, but they're not there very often. They now travel the world, doing some sightseeing but mainly visiting his kids and grandkids. Family was always his "real job". His kids don't tease him anymore, they ask him how they can raise a great family who love them and want to hang out with them and retire rich, like he did.

10 ABOUT THE AUTHOR

Shaz Jones is a #1 Best selling author on Amazon. Her latest books include:

Never Pay Bills
Nagging Success
Shortcut
Headliners
The Faithfulness Myth
Bible-based Budgets
Conversion
Atmosphere
Witness

You can visit www.ShazJones.com to find out more.